MY FIRST Little Readers

by Liza Charlesworth

For Guided Reading Level **C**

NEW YORK • TORONTO • LONDON • AUCKLAND • SYDNEY
MEXICO CITY • NEW DELHI • HONG KONG • BUENOS AIRES

Teaching Resources

The mini-books in this collection may be reproduced for classroom use. No other part of this publication may be reproduced in whole or in part, or stored in a retrieval system, or transmitted in any form or by any means, electronic, photocopying, recording, or otherwise, without written permission of the publisher. For information regarding permission, write to Scholastic Inc., 557 Broadway, New York, NY 10012-3999.

Cover design by Maria Lilja
Interior design by Grafica
Illustrations by Anne Kennedy

ISBN: 0-439-51760-5
Copyright © 2004 by Liza Charlesworth
Published by Scholastic Inc.
All rights reserved.
Printed in the U.S.A.

Contents

Introduction 4
Quick Tips for Using *My First Little Readers* 5
Easy Ideas for Extending Learning 7

Favorite Things
Lunch Crunch 15
The Pie That Jack Made 17
Clay Play 19
Bubble Shapes 21
Surprises! 23

Animal Pals
Follow That Cat! 25
Snow Tracks 27
Eight Arms Are Great 29
Counting Bugs 31
Shadow Guessing Game 33

Good for a Giggle
Polka-Dot World 35
Hot Dog, Hot Dog 37
Tail Tale 39
Funny Foods 41
Lots of Legs 43

Nonfiction Fun
Make a Pizza 45
All About Dinosaurs 47
Bat Facts 49
Monkey Business 51
Draw a Pig 53

Shapes, Sizes, and More
Round the Clown 55
Squares Are Everywhere 57
The Teeny Tiny Man 59
Giant Friends 61
This Little Piggy 63

Introduction

Welcome to *My First Little Readers: Level C*! These 25 little books were specially written to correlate with Guided Reading Level C. That means they're the perfect tools to support—and motivate—emergent readers with just a little experience under their belts. Research shows that offering children plenty of opportunities to read just-right titles boost skills and confidence, thereby setting the stage for fluency. But what constitutes *just right*? Experts agree that a book is on level when children are able to understand most of the text. And when unknown words are encountered, children are able to decode the majority of them independently with the aid of familiar strategies.

Toward that end, the titles in this set were carefully designed to match the diverse needs of the many students you teach by presenting these age-appropriate characteristics:

* one to three lines of text per page
* clear, high-support illustrations
* patterned text structure
* natural syntactic structures
* repeated and recognizable high-frequency words
* consistent print placement
* simple, familiar, engaging story lines

Although it's important for students to encounter texts at a variety of levels, reading too many easy books may inhibit kids from developing key literacy skills. And reading too many hard books often leads to feelings of frustration. However, reading a healthy number of just-right books provides children with a wealth of opportunities to be both challenged *and* successful. Via multiple experiences with on-level books, your students will be able to develop and "practice" a network of critical reading strategies including:

* predicting what will happen next in the story
* understanding characters and their motivations
* noticing the language patterns and style of the text
* figuring out unfamiliar words by using decoding skills to sound out words and context clues to confirm word meanings
* returning to the text to confirm understanding
* connecting the text to other stories and to their own lives
* forming opinions about the books they read

With this essential skills set in place, children are empowered to ascend the reading ladder with increased agility, gradually mastering more difficult titles over time—until the sky's the limit! No, fluency doesn't happen instantly, but with systematic exposure to the right books, it does happen. And that's pretty magical. The *My First Little Readers* series is here to help by providing a big boost to young learners during those all-important early years.

How to Make the Little Readers

Follow these steps to copy and put together the mini-books:

1 Remove the mini-book pages along the perforated lines. Make a double-sided copy on 8½-by-11-inch paper.

2 Cut the page in half along the solid line.

3 Place page 2 behind the title page.

4 Fold the pages in half along the dotted line. Check to be sure that the pages are in the proper order, and then staple them together along the book's spine.

NOTE: If you cannot make double-sided copies, you can photocopy single-sided copies of each page, cut apart the mini-book pages, and stack them together in order, with the title page on top. Staple the pages together along the left-hand side.

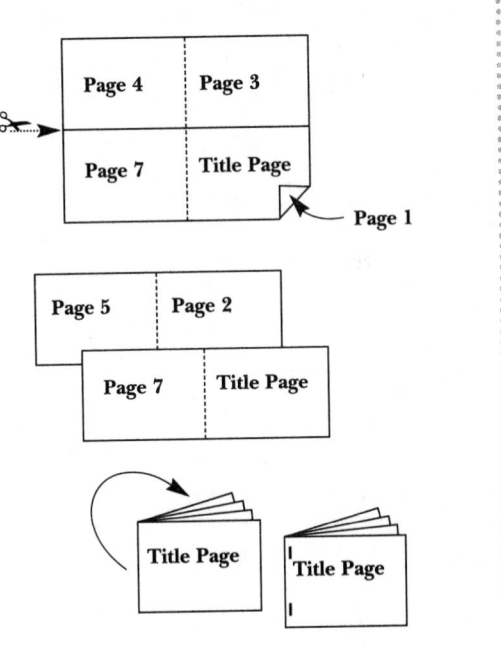

Quick Tips for Using *My First Little Readers*

Because *My First Little Readers* are reproducible, they're the perfect books to use with guided-reading groups. Following are a few quick tips on how to structure your lessons.

- **Before Reading** Introduce the book, giving students a general idea of what the story is about. Then take a picture walk through the story, inviting kids to make predictions and connect the illustrations to their own experiences. Encourage children to preview the text and find a few familiar and unfamiliar words. Discuss strategies children can use to decode unknown words, such as finding beginning or ending sounds, relying on their knowledge of word families, breaking the words into parts, or using picture cues to confirm word identification. Also, be sure to preview any concepts that may be new or challenging to children.

Connections to the Language Arts Standards

The activities in this book are designed to support you in meeting the following reading standards outlined by the Mid-continent Research for Education and Learning (McRel), an organization that collects and synthesizes national and state K–12 curriculum standards.

* Understands that print conveys meaning
* Understands how print is organized and read (e.g., identifies front and back covers, title pages, author, follows words from left to right and from top to bottom; knows the significance of spaces between words; knows the difference between letters, words, and sentences; understands the use of capitalization and punctuation as text boundaries)
* Creates mental images from pictures and print
* Uses basic elements of phonetic analysis to decode unknown words
* Understands level-appropriate sight words and vocabulary
* Uses self-correction strategies
* Reads aloud familiar stories with fluency and expression

Source—*Content Knowledge: A Compendium of Standards and Benchmarks from K–12 Education* (3rd ed.). (Mid-Continent Research for Education and Learning, 2000)

- **During Reading** Have students read the book softly to themselves as you listen in. Although children are reading independently, you are there to provide support and scaffolding. For example, you might guide kids to use word-solving strategies, such as "mining" context clues, when they get stuck. Whenever possible, try to provide prompts and encouragement without interrupting the flow of children's reading.

- **After Reading** When children have finished, discuss the reading experience. What problems did they encounter? How did they solve them? You may want to return to parts of the story that were challenging, reinforcing word-solving strategies and discussing any unfamiliar concepts or vocabulary. This is also a good time to teach a mini-lesson on word analysis. For instance, children might manipulate magnetic letters on a board to unlock a word's structure. (For example, if there are several words in the story with short -*a* spelling patterns such as -*at* and -*an*, have children build and sort these words using their magnetic letters.) After that, you can invite children to reread the story and apply their new knowledge.

- **Assessment** There are a variety of effective tools to help you assess each child's progress. To analyze a student's decoding skills, take a running record as they read. To assess comprehension, invite that child to do an oral retelling. Additionally, it often makes sense to jot down some observational notes as children read, paying close attention to where their individual challenges lie and what strategies might require reinforcement. Armed with a deep understanding of every student's strengths and weakness, you will be able to customize effective teaching plans to meet their diverse needs.

Easy Ideas for Extending Learning

Following are some quick ways to use the 25 little readers as springboards to fun activities that boost skills in reading, writing, critical thinking, math, and more.

Lunch Crunch (Class-Created Book)

Create a class book patterned on *Lunch Crunch*. Give each child a paper-bag-shaped page and this sentence to complete: *When I eat lunch, my [food] goes crunch*. (For example, a student might write, *When I eat lunch, my peanuts go crunch*.) Have students illustrate their sentences. Then, add a cover and bind the pages together with O-rings for a predictable book kids can read all by themselves.

The Pie that Jack Made (Collaborative Writing Activity)

This little book pays homage to the classic story, "The House That Jack Built." Share it with kids, then work together to write a collaborative tale based on the original. Ideas include "The Robot that Jack Built" or "The Sunflower That Jack Grew." Don't be afraid to get silly!

Clay Play (Story Sequencing)

Provide each student with *Clay Play* along with single-sided copies of the cut-apart pages (out of order and with the folios masked). Now, challenge children to use the book as a guide for placing the pages in a sequenced stack.

Bubble Shapes (Flannel Board Fun)

Cut 25 (or more) circles of varying sizes from flannel and place them on your flannel board. Now, encourage pairs of children to play with the circles and use them to create bubble objects like the ones in the little book or of their own design. To extend learning, students can use their creations as instant story starters.

Surprises! (Mystery-Box Guessing Game)

Cut three construction paper squares—one little, one medium sized, and one big—to represent boxes. Next, draw pictures of small, medium-sized, and big objects (or animals), preparing a sentence-strip clue for each. (The clue to accompany a picture of a dinosaur, for example, might be: *I used to stomp and roar, but not anymore. What am I?*) Now, place the clue in your pocket chart, secretly slipping the picture behind the big box. Read the clue together and invite volunteers to guess the answer. When someone does, celebrate by "opening" the box and revealing the hidden image.

Follow That Cat! (Purrfect Sight Word Practice)

Here's an easy way to make sight word knowledge whimsical and fun: Write 20 or so must-know sight words on index cards and place them in a pocket chart. Also, cut a cat shape from construction paper. Now, place the "cat" beside one of the word cards, exclaiming, "Follow that cat to the word that says …." Invite students to shout out the answer. Then, place the cat shape beside all the other sight words in turn.

Snow Tracks (Hands-on Science)

Why do animals and people leave tracks in the snow? On a winter day, investigate this scientific question by gathering pans of snow, then inviting kids to use plastic animals, dinosaurs, and action figures to make snow tracks. What conclusion can kids draw? Publish your findings on chart paper.

Eight Arms Are Great
(Research Connection)

It may seem amazing, but an octopus really does have eight arms! Tap kids' natural curiosity about this remarkable sea creature by demonstrating how to use a search engine to locate a child-friendly Web site to learn more about them.

Counting Bugs (Counting Creepy Crawlies)

This little book invites students to use members of the bug family to count up to five. Jot the lines of the story on chart paper, then work together to extend it to count up to the number ten. For example, for number six, you might write, *Six centipedes crawl, crawl, crawl, crawl, crawl, crawl.* When your writing is complete, promote numeracy and fluency by reading your new, improved versions together.

Shadow Guessing Game
(Shadow Show and Tell)

Give kids this enjoyable homework assignment: Use a flashlight and your fingers to invent an animal shadow, like the rabbit in the little book. The next day at school, turn off the lights and invite children to use a flashlight to share their creations and describe how to make them. If you like, award prizes for the most realistic, scary, or humorous shadows presented.

Polka-Dot World (Class Big Book)

This humorous little book imagines a world filled with polka-dotted cats and hats and bees. What are some other things that could benefit from a few polka dots? A dolphin? A dinosaur? A castle? Work together with your students to make a list—the sillier the better! Then use it to create your own big book patterned on *Polka-Dot World*.

Hot Dog, Hot Dog (Partner Read-Alouds)

Copy each line of the story (in sequence) on chart paper so it reads like a poem. Then boost fluency—and listening skills—by inviting pairs of students to perform partner reads in which they alternate reading every other line aloud. Celebrate each rendition with a rousing round of applause.

Tail Tale (Collaborative Writing Activity)

Copy the story onto chart paper. Then, fine-tune fluency by inviting groups of students to take turns reading each line round-robin style. If you like, innovate the text by inserting some original sentences such as *The leopard pulled the wart hog's tail.*

Funny Foods (Story-Building Pocket Chart)

Write each word from this little book on a separate card. Then invite groups of children to take turns "rebuilding" the story in a pocket chart. Kids can even switch the words around to create wacky food combinations such as *bananas on a hotdog.*

Lots of Legs (Animal Concentration)

Prepare two stacks of cards: one with the name and picture of each living thing from *Lots of Legs* (such as person, dog, spider), and one with the corresponding number of legs (such as 2, 4, 6). Now, invite small groups of children to shuffle the cards and place them facedown for a literacy-building game of concentration in which they match each animal with the correct number of legs.

Make a Pizza (Sequencing Practice)

Provide each student with the *Make a Pizza* little book along with single-sided copies of the cut-apart pages (out of order and with the folios masked). Then, challenge children to use the book as a guide for placing the pages in a sequenced stack.

All About Dinosaurs
(Springboard to Internet Research)

The Internet abounds with excellent Web sites devoted to dinosaur fans. Tap kids' natural curiosity about these amazing creatures by demonstrating how to use a search engine to locate a child-friendly Web site to learn more about them.

Bat Facts (Fact and Opinion Sort)

Use *Bat Facts* as a catalyst for helping children understand the meaning of the word *fact*. Jot each sentence of this book on a big index card. Then, write an equal number of bat-related opinions, for example, *I think bats are scary*, or *Bats are not nice*. Shuffle the cards, then read each one aloud, inviting students to help you sort the cards into a fact pile and an opinion pile. Then discuss the definition of fact and opinion, challenging students to come up with additions to each category.

Monkey Business (Fact-Finding Mission)

This nonfiction little book offers some facts about monkeys. But there are plenty more! Develop early research skills by using other monkey titles as well as the Internet to learn more about this remarkable mammal. Then work together to collaboratively write—and illustrate—your own Monkey Facts Big Book.

Draw a Pig
(Follow-the-Directions Art Activity)

After children have enjoyed this little book, develop direction skills by inviting them to use it as a step-by-step guide to help them draw their very own pig—just like the one in the book!

Round the Clown (Circle Scavenger Hunt)

With students, create a giant clown made completely from circle shapes. Hang it on your wall. Then, use it as a word wall to capture the names of all the things you and your students can think of that are round, such as *clock*, *pizza*, *apple*, *balloon*, and so on.

Squares Are Everywhere
(Square Scavenger Hunt)

Are squares *really* everywhere? Boost observation skills with the quick transition. Give kids one minute to silently look around the room, hunting for squares. Then, make a list of all the squares they locate. If you like, award a small prize—such as jelly beans or an extra read-aloud—if they can locate ten or more.

The Teeny Tiny Man (Story Starter)

What would life be like for the teeny tiny man in this little book? Does he have a nasty run-in with the giant mouse? Is he forced to hide beneath a thimble? Give kids a few minutes to let their imaginations run wild. Then, harness their creativity and write a collaborative story about his microscopic adventures.

Giant Friends (Fluency-Building Pocket Chart)

Copy each line from this little book on a sentence strip, inviting children to illustrate each on a big index card. Place these in your pocket chart. Then build fluency by reading your chart together, challenging volunteers to come forward and match each picture with the appropriate line.

This Little Piggy
(Write-Your-Own Nursery Rhyme)

Explain to children that this little book is "an innovation"— a new verse—on the beloved nursery rhyme of the same title. Share the classic rhyme with student, then work together to write a brand new verse patterned on the original. Publish it on chart paper to enjoy during shared reading time.

Clay Play

3

I made a lion.
It can roar!

4

I made a robot.
It can walk!

Oops!
I also made a mess.

1

See what I made out of clay.

2

I made a bird.
It can soar!

My First Little Readers • Level C   Scholastic Teaching Resources

6

I made a snake.
It can stretch!

5

I made a puppet.
It can talk!

Bubble Shapes

I can blow a bubble dragon!

I can blow a bubble wagon!

I can blow a bubble star!

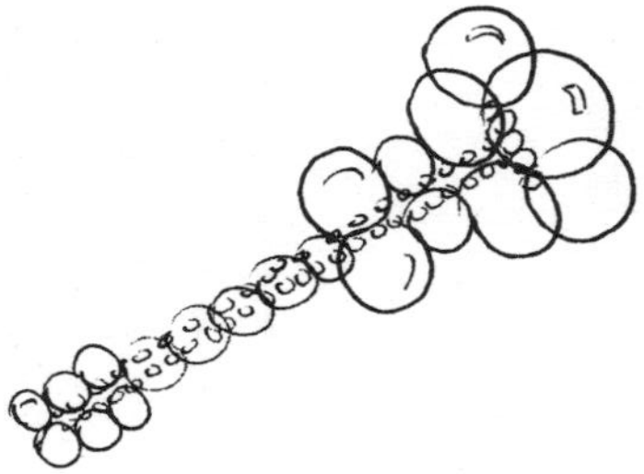

I can blow a bubble guitar!

Now my bubble fun is done!

My First Little Readers • Level C   Scholastic Teaching Resources

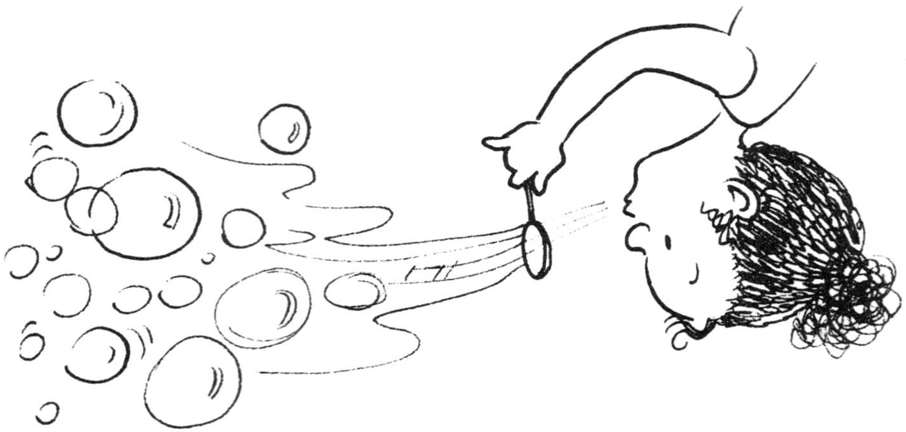

Look at the bubbles I can blow!

I can blow a bubble bear!

I can blow a bubble chair!
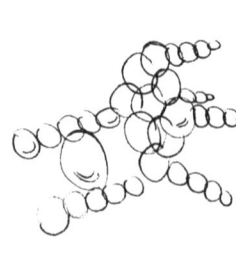
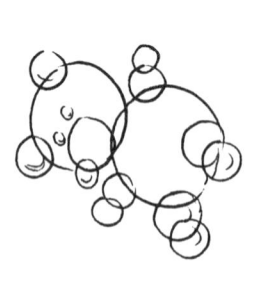

I can blow a bubble one!

I can blow a bubble sun!
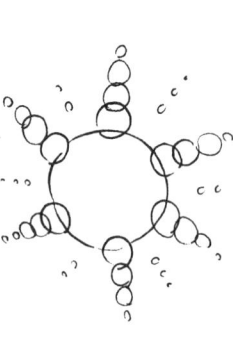

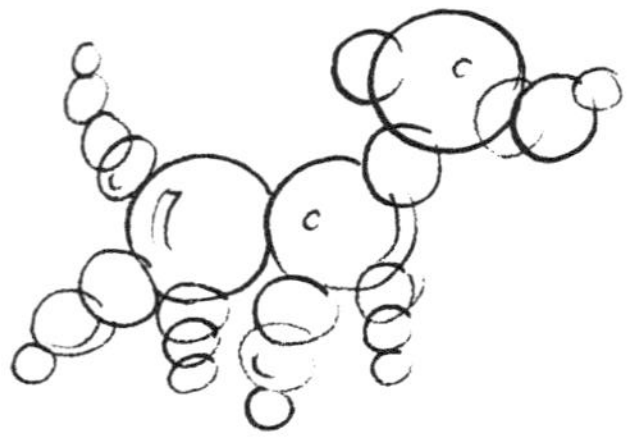

I can blow a bubble dog!

I can blow a bubble frog!

My First Little Readers • Level C   Scholastic Teaching Resources

Surprises!

Can you guess what is in this very big box?

Wow!
That is just what I wanted!

Surprise!
It is a bike.

1

Can you guess what is in this big box?

2

Surprise!
It is a computer.

My First Little Readers • Level C   Scholastic Teaching Resources

5

Can you guess what is in this very, very big box?

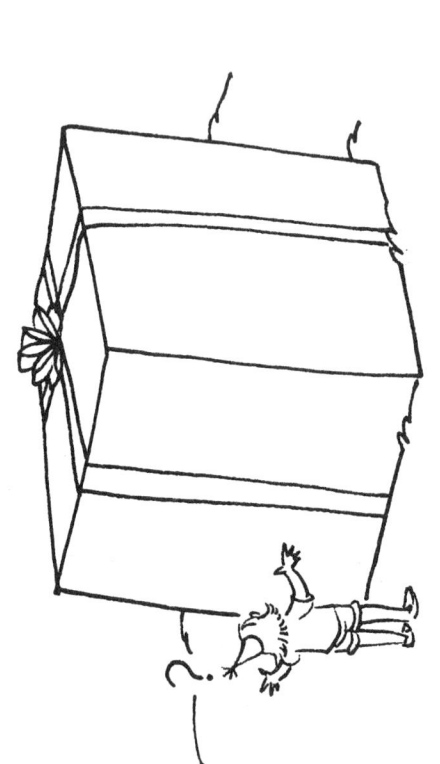

6

Surprise!
It is an elephant!

Snow Tracks

Who left these tracks in the snow?

It was a duck on the go!

Who left these tracks in the snow?

It was a kid on the go!

Who left these tracks in the snow?

It was a fox on the go!

My First Little Readers • Level C   Scholastic Teaching Resources

1

Who left these tracks in the snow?

It was a horse on the go!

2

Who left these tracks in the snow?

It was a deer on the go!

My First Little Readers • Level C   Scholastic Teaching Resources

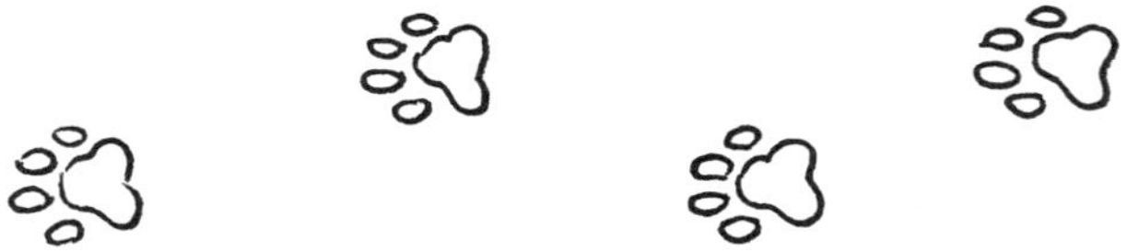

6

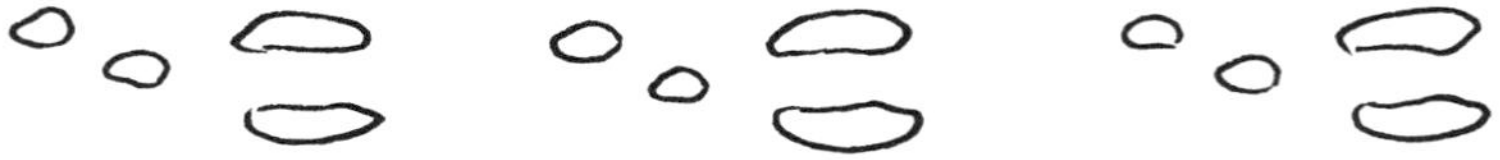

Who left these tracks in the snow?

It was a rabbit on the go!

5

Who left these tracks in the snow?

It was a dog on the go!

Eight Arms Are Great

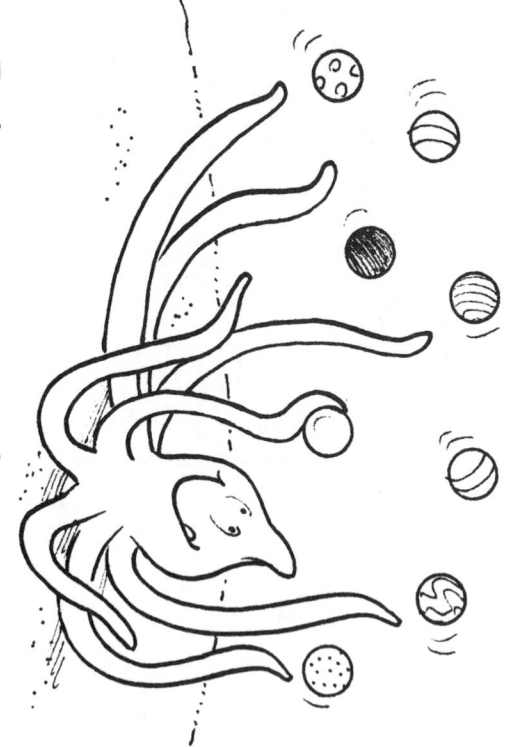

Eight arms are great for juggling balls!

My First Little Readers • Level C   Scholastic Teaching Resources

Eight arms are great for eating fruit!

Good-bye!

Eight arms are great for waving good-bye!

Eight arms are great!

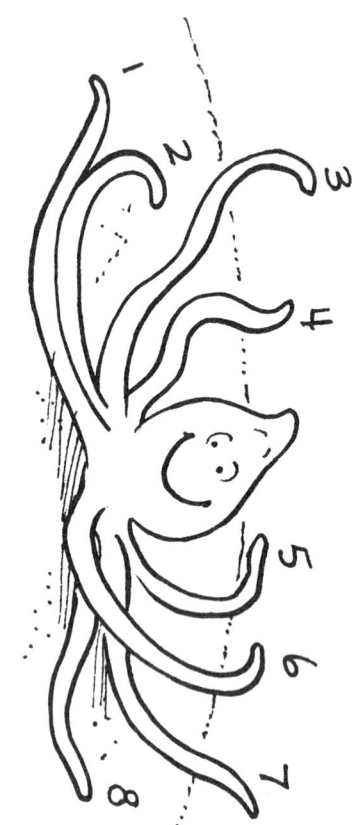

Eight arms are great for reading books!

My First Little Readers • Level C   Scholastic Teaching Resources

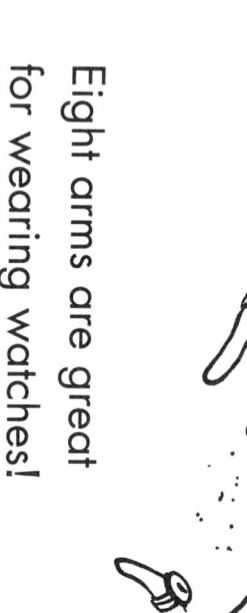

Eight arms are great for wearing watches!

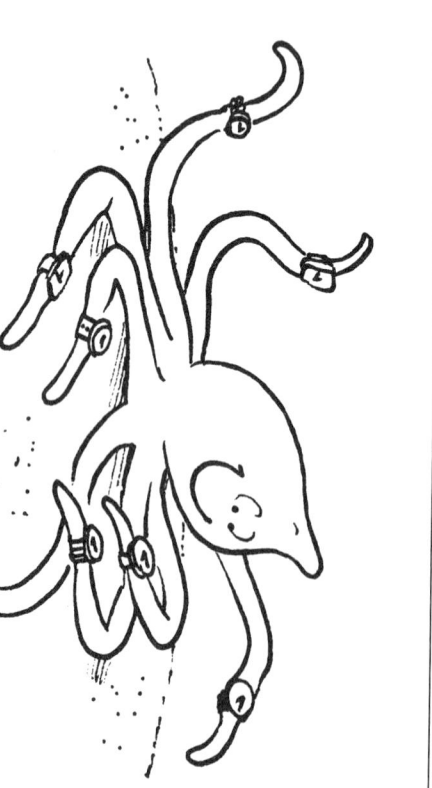

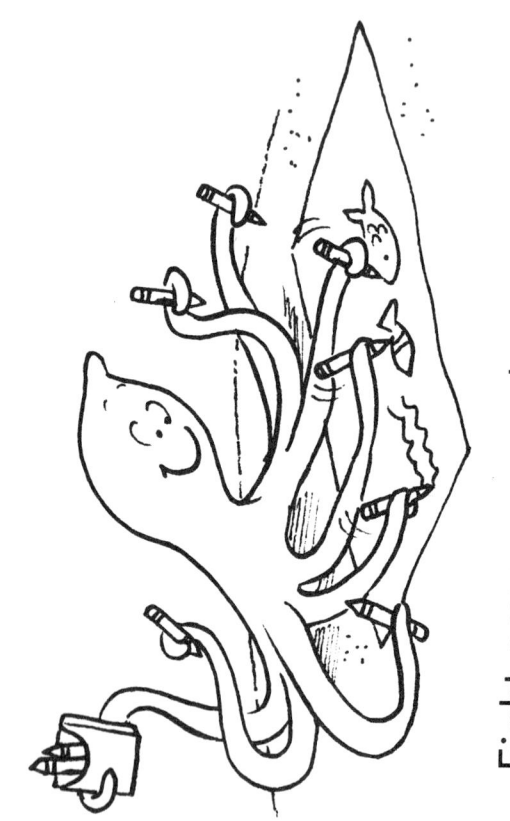

Eight arms are great for drawing pictures!

Counting Bugs

Two butterflies flutter, flutter.

Three worms wiggle, wiggle, wiggle.

But none of them makes a single peep!

Let's count bugs in my garden.

One grasshopper hops.

My First Little Readers • Level C   Scholastic Teaching Resources

Five spiders creep, creep, creep, creep.

Four ladybugs fly, fly, fly, fly.

Shadow Guessing Game

3

Guess what made this shadow?

7

Here is how you do it.
Want to try?

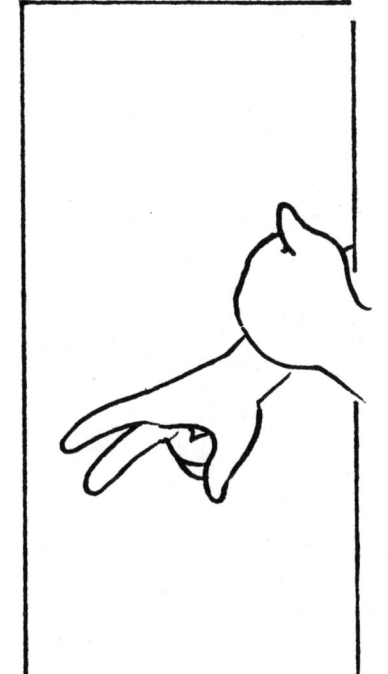

My First Little Readers • Level C   Scholastic Teaching Resources

---

4

Did you guess a snake?
You are right!

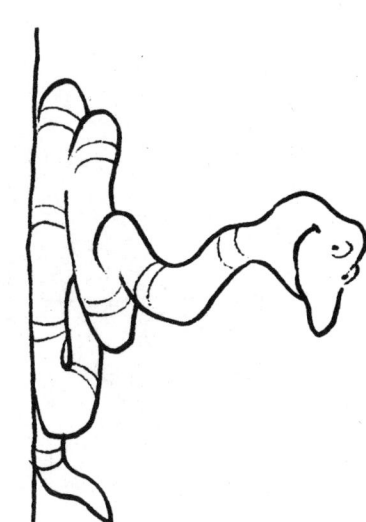

Guess what made this shadow?

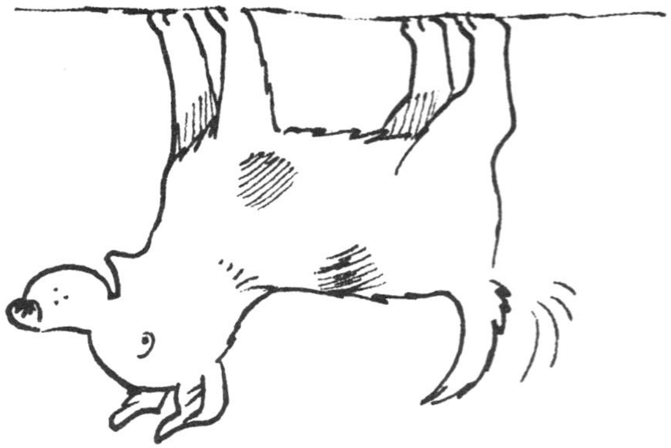

Did you guess a dog?
You are right!

Guess what made this shadow?

Did you guess a rabbit?
You are wrong.
It was only my fingers.

Polka-Dot World

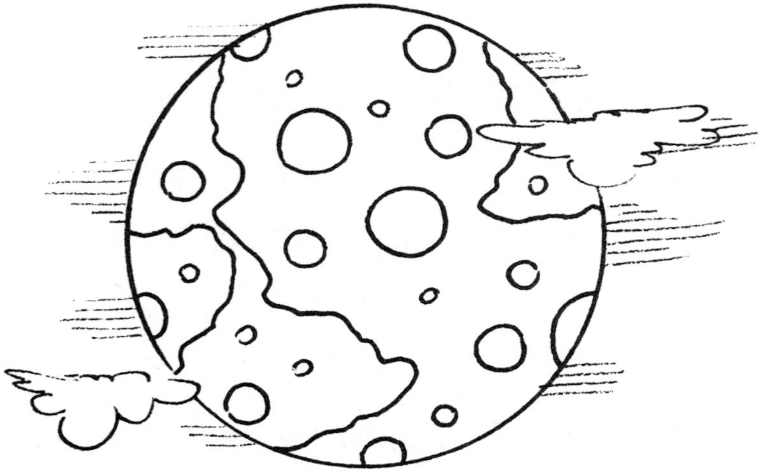

There are polka dots on this cake!

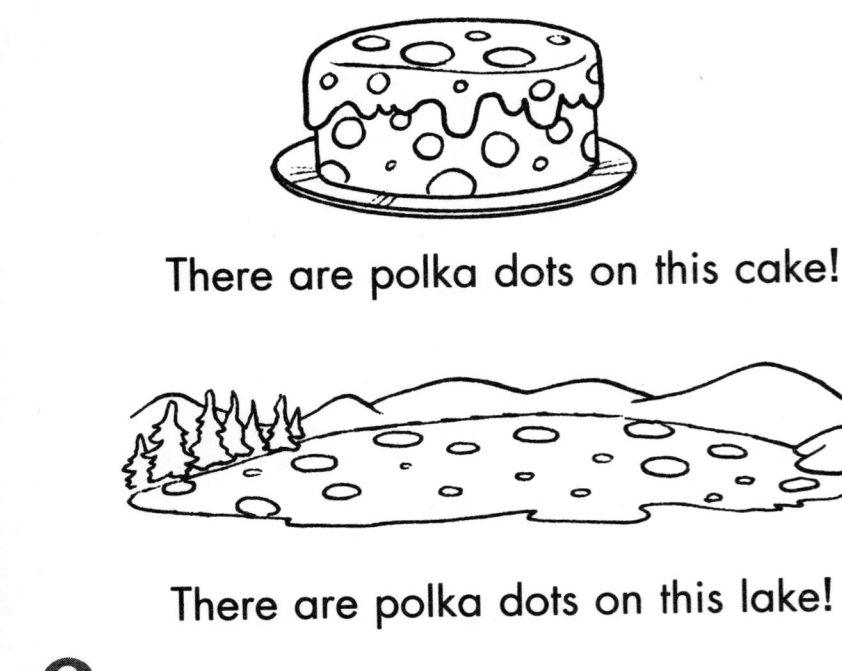

There are polka dots on this lake!

There are polka dots on this dog!

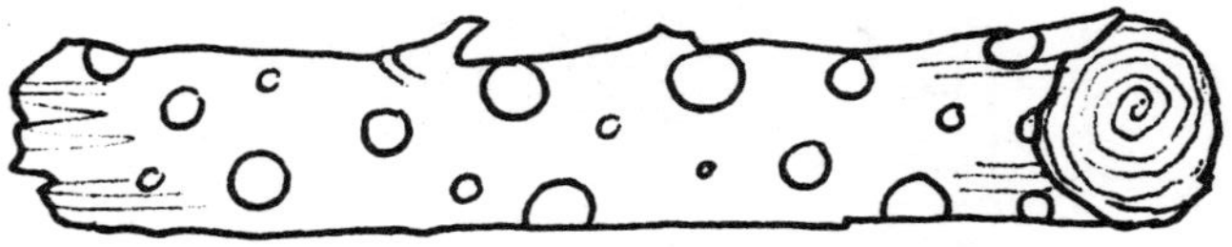

There are polka dots on this log!

There are polka dots on this bee!

There are even polka dots on me!

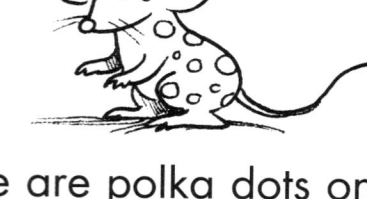

1
There are polka dots on this house!

There are polka dots on this mouse!

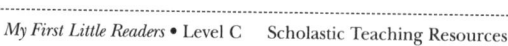

2
There are polka dots on this fish!

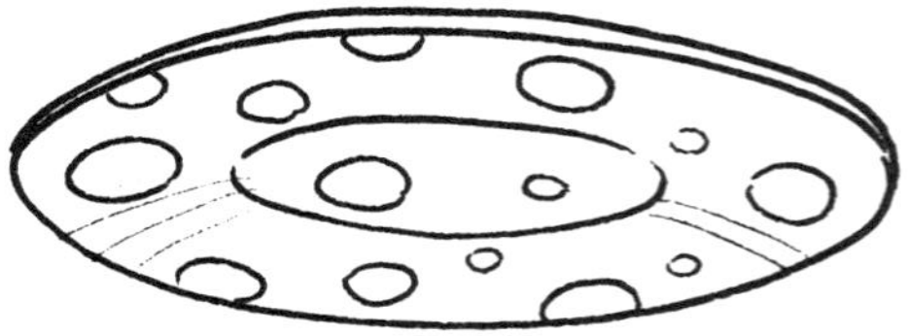

There are polka dots on this dish!

5
There are polka dots on this rug!

There are polka dots on this mug!

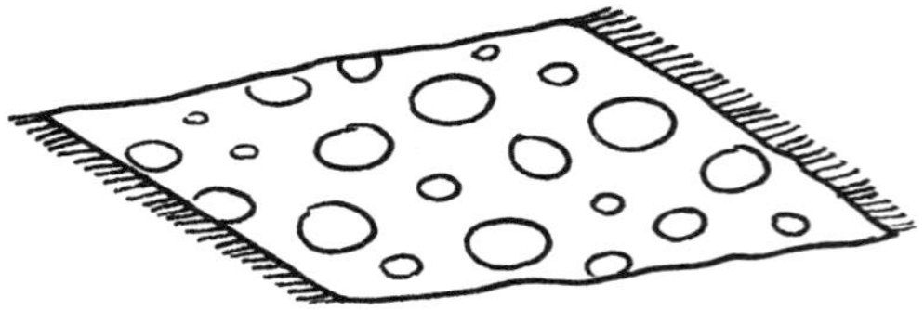

6
There are polka dots on this box!

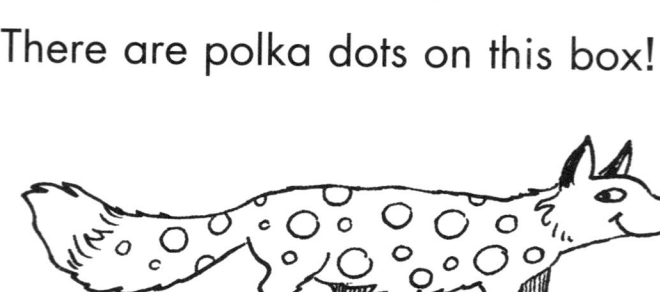

There are polka dots on this fox!

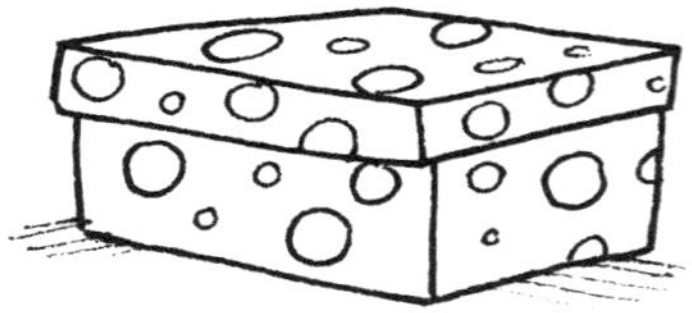

My First Little Readers • Level C   Scholastic Teaching Resources

Hot Dog, Hot Dog

French fries, french fries on my plate,
boy, oh, boy, you sure look great!

Salad, salad on my plate,
boy, oh, boy, you sure look great!

Nothing, nothing on my plate,
boy, oh, boy, my tummy aches!

My First Little Readers • Level C   Scholastic Teaching Resources

Hot dog, hot dog on my plate,
boy, oh, boy, you sure look great!

Hamburger, hamburger on my plate,
boy, oh, boy, you sure look great!

Cookie, cookie on my plate,
boy, oh, boy, you sure look great!

Watermelon, watermelon on my plate,
boy, oh, boy, you sure look great!

Tail Tale

Then alligator pulled giraffe's tail.
Ouch!

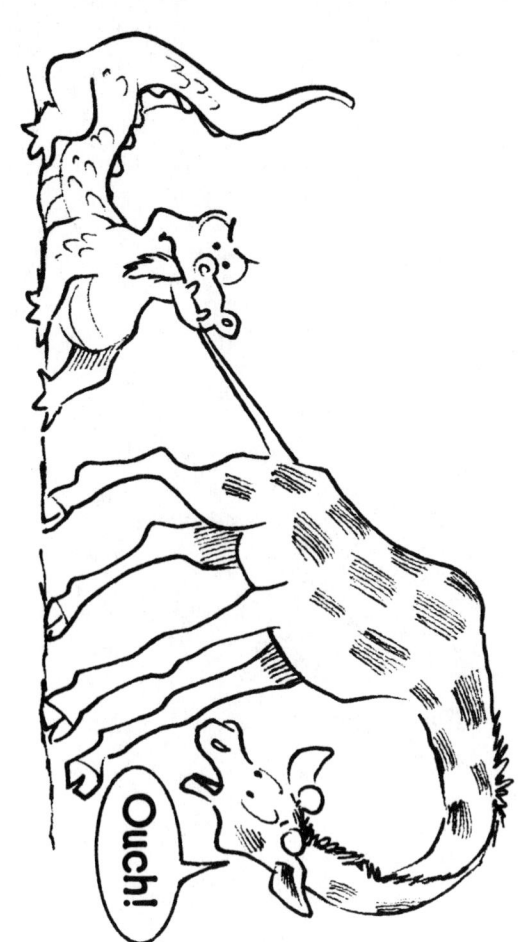

Then giraffe pulled peacock's tail.
Ouch!

Then tiger pulled monkey's tail.
Do you think that was fair?
Ouch!

My First Little Readers • Level C   Scholastic Teaching Resources

1

Monkey pulled zebra's tail.

2

Then zebra pulled alligator's tail.

My First Little Readers • Level C   Scholastic Teaching Resources

Then snake pulled tiger's tail.

6

Then peacock pulled snake's tail.

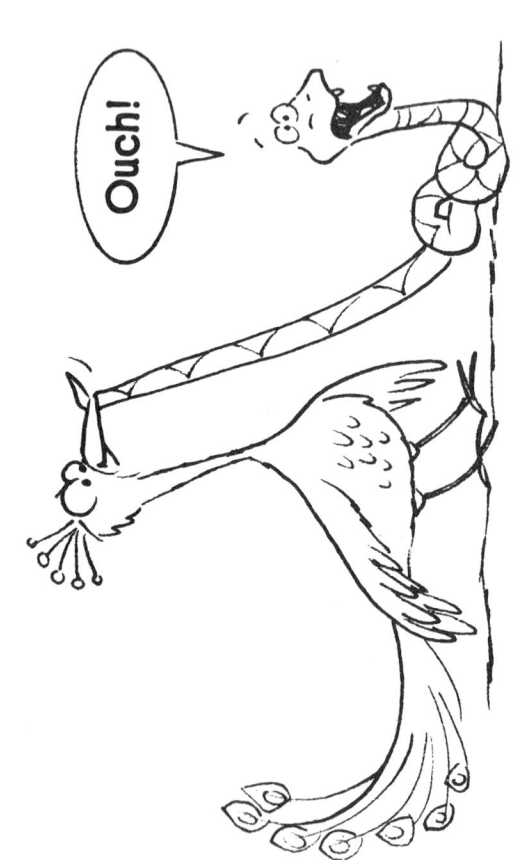

5

Funny Foods

He likes carrots on his cupcake.
Yucky, yucky!

He likes sugar on his sandwich.
Yucky, yucky!

He likes ice cream in his tummy!
Yummy, yummy!

My First Little Readers • Level C   Scholastic Teaching Resources

Page 1

He like pickles on his pizza.
Yucky, yucky!

Page 2

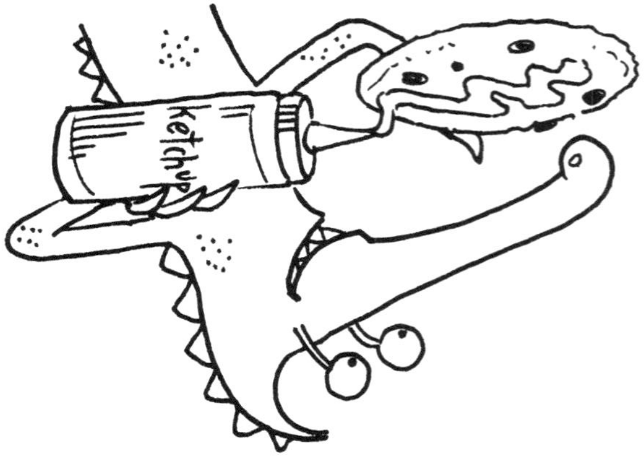

He likes ketchup on his cookie.
Yucky, yucky!

Page 5

He likes bananas on his burger.
Yucky, yucky!

Page 6

He likes honey on his hotdog.
Yucky, yucky!

My First Little Readers • Level C   Scholastic Teaching Resources

Lots of Legs

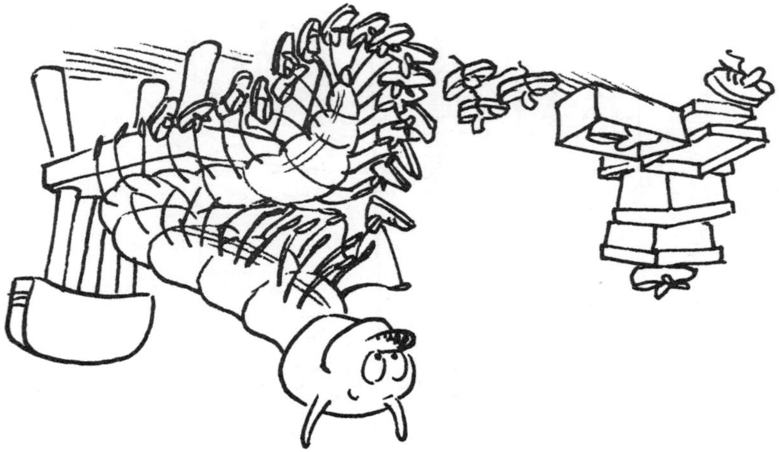

How many legs does a horse have?

A horse has 4 legs.

How many legs does an ant have?

An ant has 6 legs.

My, oh, my!
That is a lot of shoes to tie!

My First Little Readers • Level C   Scholastic Teaching Resources

1

How many legs does a snake have?

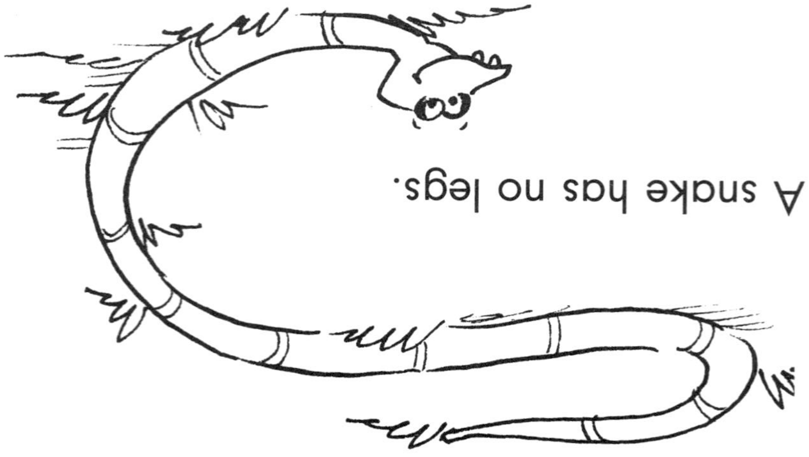

A snake has no legs.

2

How many legs does a girl have?

A girl has 2 legs.

5

How many legs does a spider have?

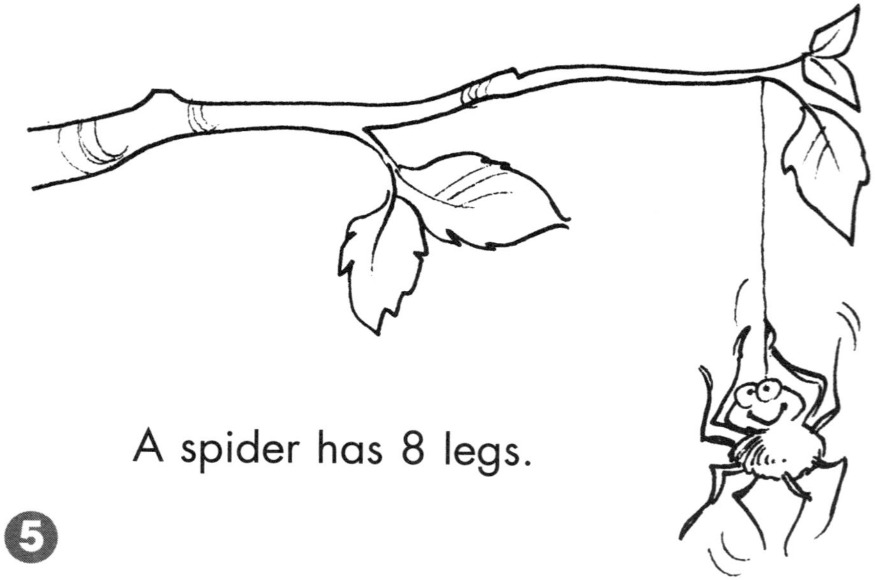

A spider has 8 legs.

6

How many legs does a centipede have?

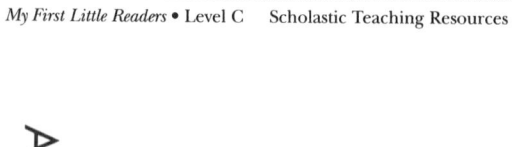

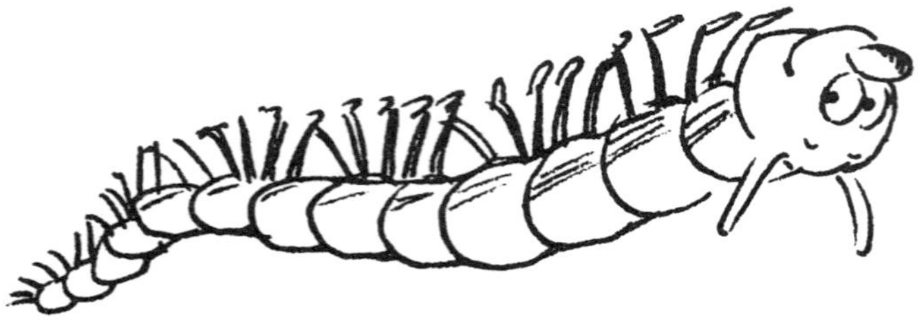

A centipede has 30 legs.

My First Little Readers • Level C   Scholastic Teaching Resources

Make a Pizza

Step two:
Put on the sauce.

Step three:
Put on the spice.

All done!
May I have some, please?

1

Let's make a pizza.
There are five steps.

2

Step one:
Roll out the dough.

My First Little Readers • Level C   Scholastic Teaching Resources

6

Step five:
Put it in the oven.

5

Step four:
Put on the cheese.

All About Dinosaurs

Some dinosaurs ate leaves.

Some dinosaurs ate meat.

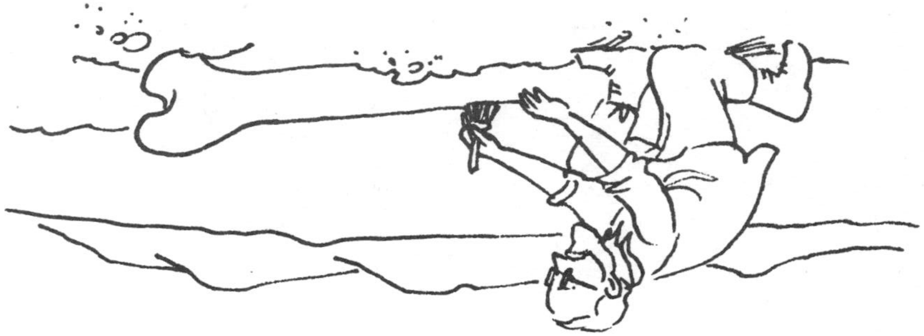

How do we know?
Some dinosaurs left bones behind for us to find!

1

Some dinosaurs had spikes.

My First Little Readers • Level C   Scholastic Teaching Resources

2

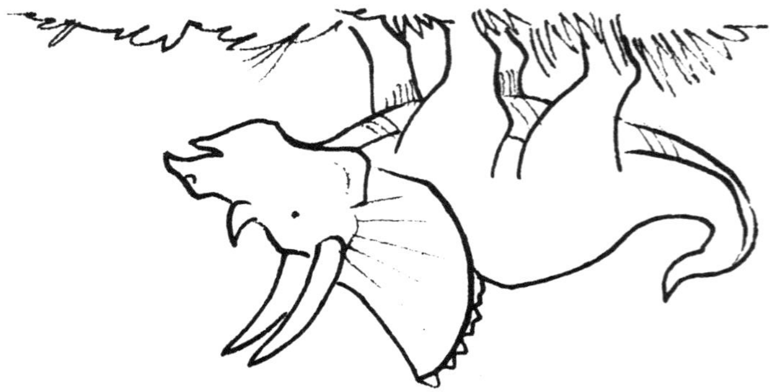

Some dinosaurs had horns.

5

Some dinosaurs were as big as a bus.

6

Some dinosaurs were as small as a chicken.

Bat Facts

Bats sleep upside down.
That is a fact!

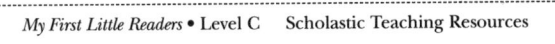

Bats look for food at night.
That is a fact!

Bats are amazing.
That is a fact!

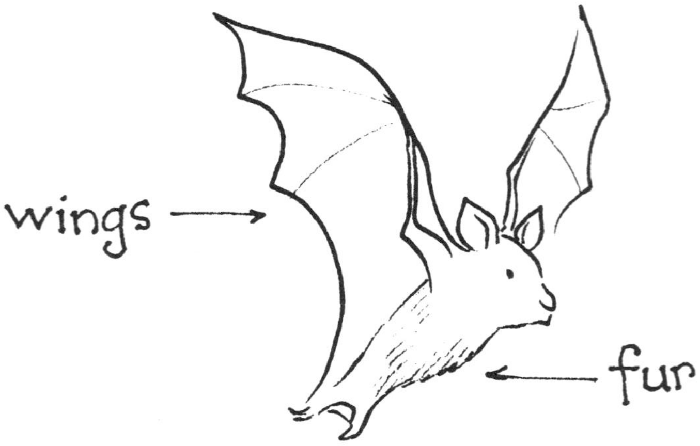

Bats have wings and fur.
That is a fact!

wings
fur

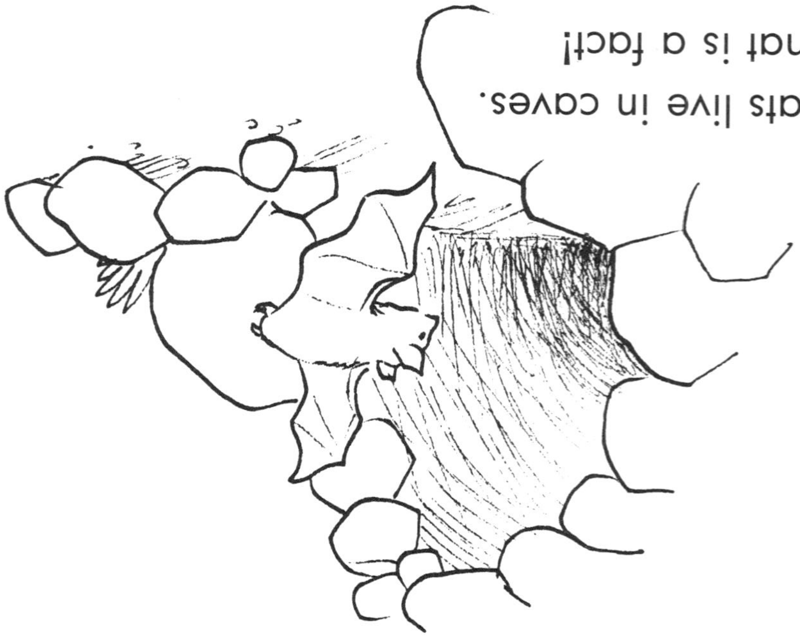

Bats live in caves.
That is a fact!

My First Little Readers • Level C   Scholastic Teaching Resources

Bats clean themselves like cats.
That is a fact!

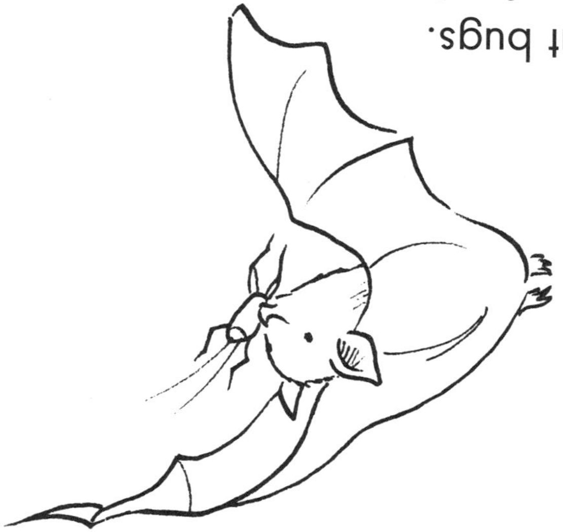

Bats eat bugs.
That is a fact!

Monkey Business

Monkeys like to swing in trees.

Monkeys like to sleep in trees.

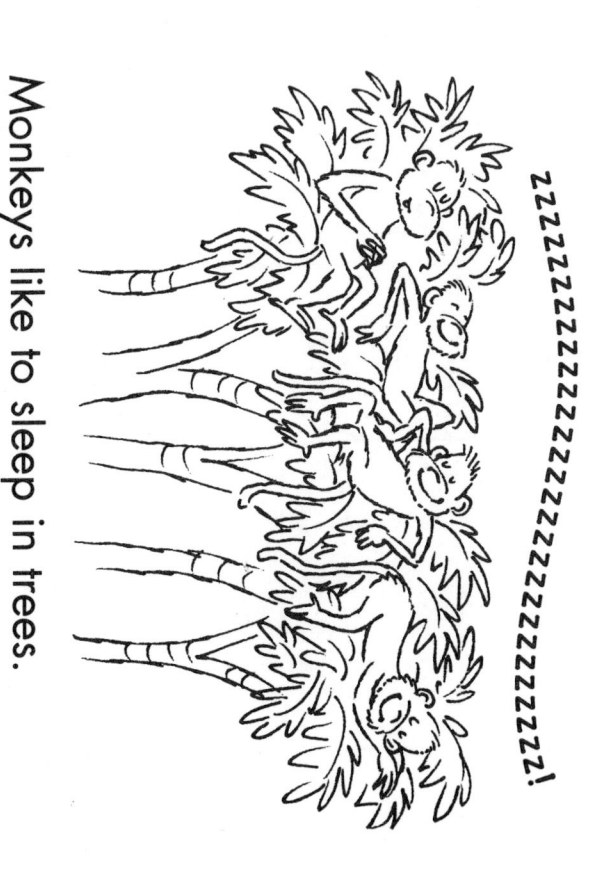

But monkeys do not like itchy fleas!

My First Little Readers • Level C   Scholastic Teaching Resources

1

Want to learn what monkeys like?

2

Monkeys like to live in groups.

My First Little Readers • Level C   Scholastic Teaching Resources

6

Monkeys like to say "Eee-eee!"

5

Monkeys like to eat bananas.

Round the Clown

③
His ball is round.
That is right!

④
His balloon is round.
That is right!

⑦
His lollipop is not round now.
That is right!

Crunch!

My First Little Readers • Level C   Scholastic Teaching Resources

1

Here is a clown.
His name is Round.

Hi! I'm Round.

2

His nose is round.
That is right!

5

His hoop is round.
That is right!

6

His lollipop is round.
That is right.

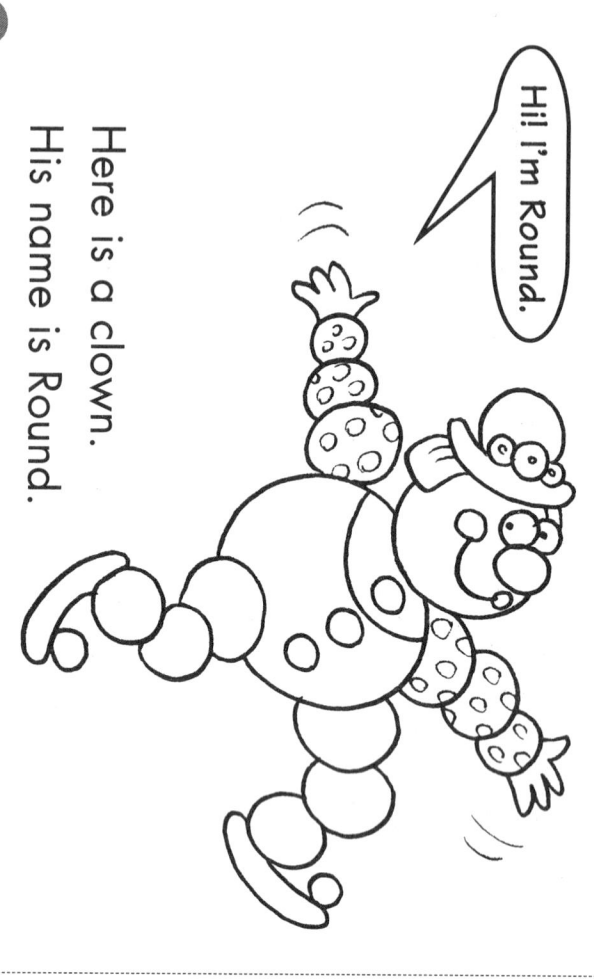

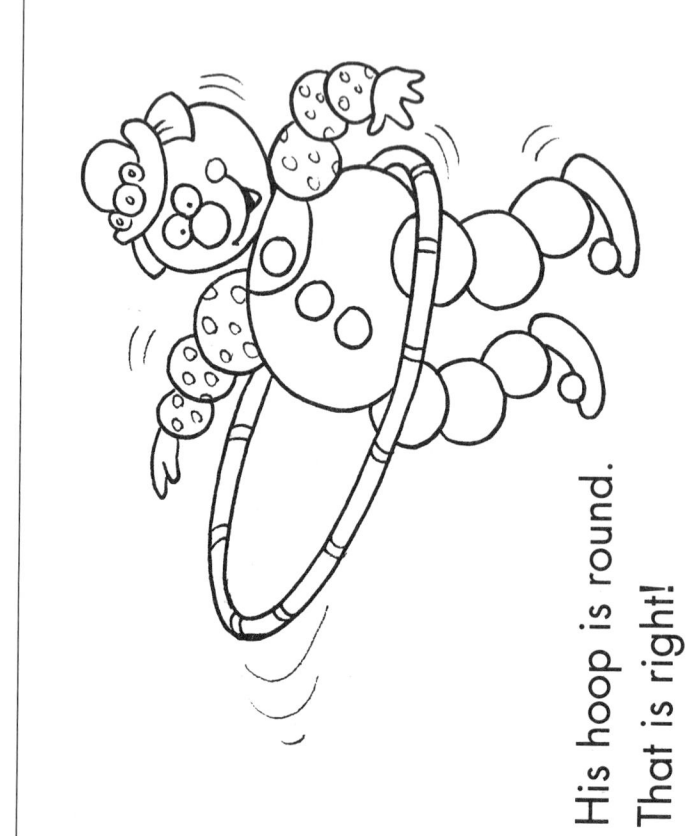

My First Little Readers • Level C   Scholastic Teaching Resources

Squares Are Everywhere

3

There are three squares on this jar.
Can you find them?

4

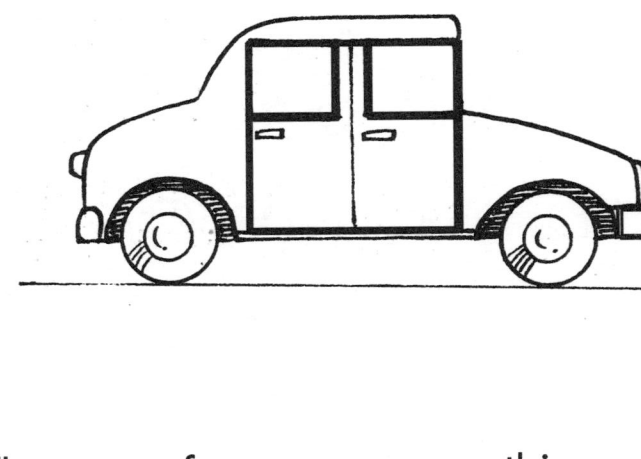

There are four squares on this car.
Can you find them?

7

Squares are everywhere!
Can you find them?

1

There is one square on this bear.
Can you find it?

2

There are two squares on this chair.
Can you find them?

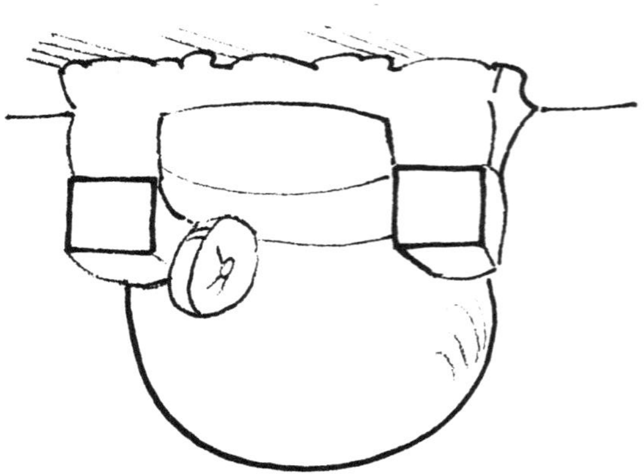

My First Little Readers • Level C   Scholastic Teaching Resources

5

There are five squares on this shelf.
Can you find them?

6

There are six squares on this elf.
Can you find them?

The Teeny Tiny Man

This is his teeny tiny son.

My name is Ted!

This is his teeny tiny daughter.

My name is Sue!

right next door to a GIANT mouse!

1

This is a teeny tiny man.

"Hello!"

2

This is his teeny tiny wife.

"Nice to meet you!"

5

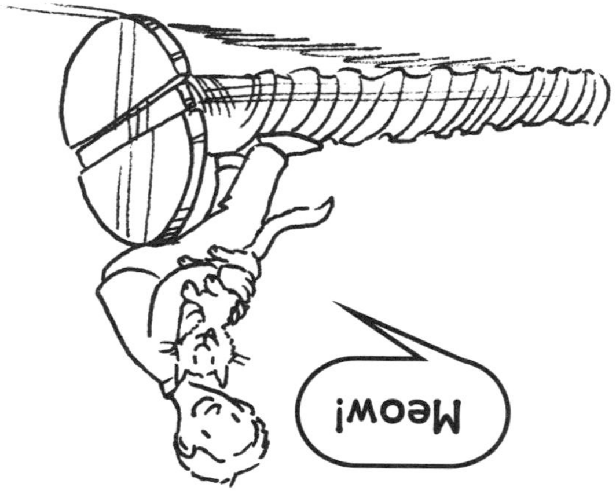

This is his teeny tiny cat.

"Meow!"

6

They all live together in this teeny tiny house …

"This is our home."

My First Little Readers • Level C   Scholastic Teaching Resources

Giant Friends

I met a giant that was as tall as a house.

I met a giant that was as tall as a building.

It was hard for him to shake hands with me!

My First Little Readers • Level C   Scholastic Teaching Resources

1

I met a giant that was as tall as a giraffe.

2

I met a giant that was as tall as a tree.

My First Little Readers • Level C   Scholastic Teaching Resources

5

I met a giant that was as tall as a mountain.

6

And as you can see...

This Little Piggy

This little piggy ate some popcorn.

This little piggy curled her hair.

up in the air.

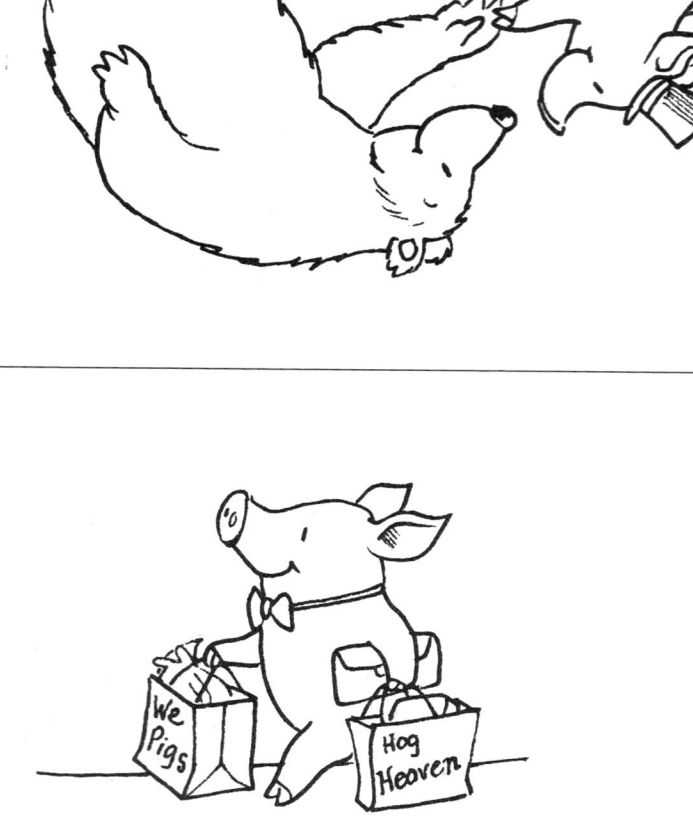

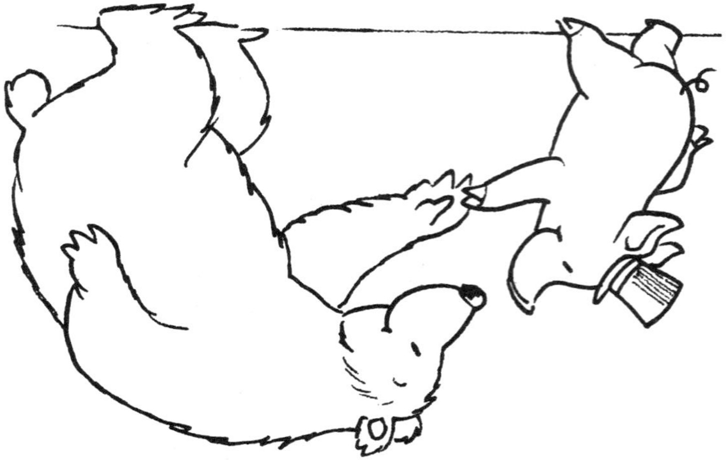

1

This little piggy went out shopping.

2

This little piggy met a bear.

My First Little Readers • Level C   Scholastic Teaching Resources

6

wee, wee, wee

5

And this little piggy went